D1738082

For the hands that hold me

Contents

Preface

"For me there is only the traveling on paths that have heart, on any path that may have heart, and the only worthwhile challenge is to traverse its full length--and there I travel looking, looking breathlessly."

-Carlos Castaneda, The Teachings of Don Juan:
A Yaqui Way of Knowledge

What you hold in your hands is the product of my experiences. Stories of friends and family that have touched my life. In the pages to follow it is my sincere hope that you can take what speaks to you and leave the rest.

Christian
San Francisco
October 2018

'Regalo'
-

I grew up in my grandfather's home
Under his roof every holiday was a parade of pan dulce
And Thanksgiving dinner
Camping trips
Smiling faces
Poker chips
Nintendo 64 and hide and go seek.
-

But grandfather passed away when I was 7 years old
And for many years my family was left trying to pick up the pieces-
In those days Christmas Eve tamales felt much lonelier.
-

But what I found was something beautiful
That grandfather's legacy lives on
Through the roots of this family tree
His children
That every tia y tio
Now turned abuela y abuelo, as years passed has their own traditions
Their own Christmas Eve tamales.
-

That we still comeback to grandfathers' home on Christmas day
Sharing hard earned tamales & old war stories of the man
And this: a parting gift made metaphor for life and death
Of an ending giving rise to new beginnings
This may have been the single greatest lesson he left me with.
-

'Nopalito'

El Nopal, que crece
Las raíces – las venas del desierto

Ni importa, cuándo hace calor ni frío
Ni le importa a el Nopal el hambre o la sed

Toca el cielo: sus flores
Brillantes estrellas
Del desierto sueños

Sigue Nopalito, sigue
Creciendo
Respirando
y
Florecer
Con ojos tan abiertos

-Casa de los abuelos

Nopalito

The Nopal, that grows
Your roots – the veins of desert

No matter, when it is hot or cold
Nor the hunger or thirst

Touch the sky: your flowers
Brilliant stars
Of desert dreams

Forward Nopalito, forward
Growing
Breathing
&
Bloom
With eyes wide open

-Grandparent's house

'*Medio*'

To live in the Borderlands means you
Crecer como un contradicción andando
Hablando mentiras y media verdades
Tu eres de aqui, but not really
In their eyes nor your own you will always be a stranger
But you are so much more than this scorched earth.

To live in the Borderlands means knowing that you carry
The weight of ancestors in your chest
Bones hanging like low hanging fruit
Cracking and grinding like graveyard.

Cuando vives en la Frontera
You are caught working, loving & dying in the middle
Donde cultura, guerra, oro y paz cross paths
When the crashing of *tequila* bottles
Echoes like bombshells, shake your family down to the foundation
Lo mismo que ha estado sucediendo por generaciones.

Para sobrevivir por la Frontera
You had to kill your voice, your culture, your customs
The dreams of parents, lost to deserts
Like heart sick: cracked, dried out
Hollow whispers of dust, nightmare, flesh & blood
Scattered to the borderlands
This fate not set in stone.

Para florecer en esa tierra olvidado
You will need to pick up the pieces
Sharpen your thorns
Water your own garden
Carve out a space
Stand tall and take things
One day at a time.

'Building 520 C'

Palo Alto
Searching for answers late at night
30 minutes before lights out

He is like, like
Like a ghost
Like a whisper
His voice is raspy
Like he is a thousand miles away
Asking

     " Christian why are you up so early? Christian, Christian, Christian is everything okay?

-I remind him its 9:32 pm
But he doesn't get it
                           "But Christian its so earlyyy..."
                             -"Its night time dad"
                                 "Oh"
He sounds drowsy
                      "All the meds they have me on son"

-I ask how he is
He tells me that
                       "Oh I'll be out in two weeks,
Once they make me better, not like I am but me like I was"
                     "This isn't me"   he says
"This me now, no they are going to make me like I was, I was before,
                       Not like I am now."

He starts breaking down,
                     "I love you Christian,
How is the hurting on the inside – the heart?"   -He asks
                     "How are you doing?"

And my heart is cracking into pieces: I feel like saw dust
But I don't tell him that
                     "I'm fine dad
                     I'm fine"
"That's good, get some rest I am sooo tired Christian
                     I love you son"
                     -"I love you too dad"

                     Click
                     "Oh father..."
And I proceed to cry.

'4'

My father is screaming
He cannot control it
Frustration pouring out of him like a fire hydrant
He a mountain of a man
And I feel so very very small
And afraid
I do not understand
The sun of my life is bursting
His Temper paints nightmares along my bedroom walls
Our apartment become a battlefield
-I left with This purple heart I never asked for
Yet
When the storm subsides
He gets on one knee looks me in the eyes and swears he will never lay a hand on me
And I believe him.

6:
He tells me when he clung to life by a shoestring
I saved his life
Long hopeless months in the hospital
When the doctors told him he would never walk again
I gave him something worth fighting for.

8:
They take me away from him
They say I cannot see him anymore
I cry every night
I do not understand
So many questions
And poking
And prodding
Their questions make me feel dirty
Like I did something wrong?
But nothing ever happened.

10:
My father at 54 years old tells me
That if he died tomorrow
That would be okay
Living off borrowed time-
He's had plenty of life he says
He says he wasn't a kind man
That he did bad things
He hurt people
But father

I tell him, life is not black and white
And you are a good man
In my eyes
The kindest soul
I've ever known
He tells me we will talk about it more when I'm older.

13:
Grandma passes away, he has no family left
Only me.

15: I choose to live at my mom's house.

15: my dad moves away.

15: things felt so much easier that way.

18:
Father is homeless now
Older
Weathered face
And sullen shoulders
He's always sick
He hates the shelter.

He tells me he almost shot himself in Reno
About broken marriages
And his daughter he doesn't speak to anymore
He tells me about selling cocaine
And how to survive in this world.

21:
His hands are shaking
He speaks of
Vietnam
Soldiers killing children
American GI beheaded in front of him in jungle half way around the world
He saw it all
Late night conversations
He sounds raspy
Like he is a thousand miles away.

He breaks down
And I never knew how to help him
But I am here

And father I will always be here for you.

Today: I am 21
A stranger to this family name
My father teaches me how to be a man
To look you in the eyes when I shake your hand
That my word is my bond
And you never, ever hit a woman
He teaches me patience
About mental health
& unconditional love
And my need for balance.

My entire life I've grappled with the pushing and pulling of our tides
Needing to know the man
The side that raised me
Loving me unconditional
On my worst days
When I least deserved it
I pushed him away
Bent on not duplicating his same Mistakes.

But what if
What if the more things changed
The more they stayed the same
I am just left here picking up the pieces.

'Growing Pains'
-

Living out a dream of mine
From a young age I wanted nothing more than to leave and run far far away but
As it turns out that wasn't all I thought it was cracked up to be.
-

It wasn't as if I could keep running from my problems forever
Not as if putting half a planets distance between us would automatically make me happy
And yet it did!
If only for a short time...
Or at least that's what I kept telling myself
As I chased a sense of warmth
Of belonging at the bottom of a bottle
Letting go in a bar thousands of miles away with some people I didn't know.
-

But the truth is there is no quick fix
No 99 ¢ cent solution
The truth is to be happy I had to find my peace
I thought my year abroad would be the single greatest experience of my life
And it has been
But
It has also been the hardest
Growing pains
As everything I ever held dear fell away
My friends
My family
My home
I was left alone caving in on myself.
-

The truth is some days I feel like I am drowning
Choking on my own inability
Yet other days
I can feel a great fire rising up from within my chest
Devouring me
As the sun and stars burst
Cascading me across the sky
Strewn out along the constellations.
-

The truth is I am but the ocean and her tides
Calm
Resting
Waiting
Yet in the same instance I am the beach
Yearning for futures yet unseen
Sand grains broken and scattered to the winds

Like so much stardust.
-

I've learned that happiness lives and breathes within myself
It's born in the moments that take my breath away
And the laughter which washes away the anxiety.
-

The truth is I have found my voice here
And it is the tool with which I fight to find my happiness inside of myself
Everyday.
-

'Soñador'

I had a dream last night
In it I'm remembering futures yet unseen
When I ask myself
-

What about when the rolling of waves
Became the passing of days
Where we could just sit on hilltops watching as
Fog rolled itself from minutes unto days
Where silence kissed
The earth
&
Providence sang us to sleep at night.

'How many ways to say'

"Don't stay up too late"
She says.

On instinct I reply
"I won't"
But I will.

She's been saying this since I was in 6th grade
The first impulse a rush of annoyance
And yet.

Another part of me
A part that has tasted just enough of life
Of endings
Changing and becomings.

Knows that nothing can last forever
And I am grateful
For these words.

How many ways to say I love you
Without saying I love you
Time please stop sliding through my fingers so fast.

'Mama'

My mother has the ability to light up the room
Warm your heart with her smile
She is kind
Outspoken
Humble
She is genuine
But she is also shy & a bit self-conscious.

My mother is beautiful
But somedays she has a hard time seeing that.

But when mom steps out to dance
We all stop and stare
She says
"Mijo lets dance salsa"
So, I spin her salsa
As she smiles this huge cheesy smile and laughs
And laughs
And laughs
And in that moment
She feels beautiful.

'Notes from *La Clínica*'

Our patients are teaching me humility
They've shown me our constant reality made flesh & blood It is not always pretty
But it is true, rooted & real.

They've touched my life in deep and impactful ways
Some days I come home and want to cry
None of it is fair.
This empire of trauma
These systems that bind us
So many broken brown bodies.

A student to their struggle,
I am made speaker for the dead
Dead dreams, and dying bodies.
Today he is like a lesson
Like smoldering ash.
Homeless, self-medicating, malnutrition
Alcoholism your warmest hug.
You told me you have had this ongoing headache for two years
The pain prevents you from sleeping,
But it won't improve without sleep.
As I come to understand your pain
My heart sinks, I do not have the answers
What if I told you I cannot help you.

You drink so much that the Tylenol would
Smash your liver
More harm than good.
I asked you what a "drink" meant in your book
You admitted a drink was "maybe 12 or 15 beers"
Cases and cases of *caguamas*
Not normal sized, the big ones.
None of this is new, I've heard this many time before
From many different faces.
We cannot give you an Ibuprofen for the pain
Because you never know for sure when or from where your next hot meal will come from.
The doctor in our *Clínica* says that GI tract bleeding is a real concern here
That it would be irresponsible to prescribe given your context.
I sit listening to the medical students and Doctor
I'm looking for answers in their faces
But everywhere I turn I recognize a resignation
This is a failure of the system they say
Without saying,
There is no magic fix
I sit back and sigh.

You came in with a nail in your foot
We said it didn't look infected but please we are just students
Please just, just wait for the doctor to take a look
But
I could see the beginnings of withdrawal
Rocking back and forth
Anxious, tense jaw,
It was in your eyes.
You left
I pleaded with you to Stay,
Stay in the *Clínica, La Doctora* will see you only in a short while.
You said yes, promised, just step out for a drink to calm the nerves.
You never did come back,
Never answered my calls
Matter of fact I never did see you again
I took it home with me that day
But we are here-
La Clínica
When you're ready.

Clínica opens at 8 a.m.
It's 8:05 in our circle
Our *círculo* like a waiting room Like a confessional
A safe space.
I want to make small talk
I ask about her necklace
It's beautiful
"does it have a meaning?"
I ask

"pues sí"

gazing away she says- *"Mi hijo"*
...he was murdered not long ago
Near his home
She explains
As she began to cry.
Su Compañera wraps her arms around her,
Her husband recently passed away too
You find strength in each other's arms
En Nuestro Círculo.

A quiet woman sits on the edge of our círculo
Mirando
Escuchando

She begins to speak.
Explaining how
She was deported
Crossed *La Frontera* back
How *Los Coyotes* held her in a room made prison cell for twenty days
She still has the same shoes on
The floors were disgusting she explains
Dark rooms,
They fed her but once a day
She could not bring herself to eat.
She's been coming to our *Clínica* to work through things
She cut her hair, dyed color.
As a *Clínica,* we put some money together
Bought her a new pair of shoes.
One of my favorite moments,
Her face when she slipped out of those same old shoes
She had on through it all.
Ella cayó, llorando
It was a small thing, but to her, it meant the world.

How do I tell you?
No tengo las palabras
You did everything right
Everything you could
But I am sorry you are not prediabético anymore
You have type 2 diabetes.

But I'm not the one that has to tell you that
That's the Doctor's job
Silencio
The patient room is quiet.
When your wife not missing a beat
Chimes in that things will be okay
Her smile, her warmth
Su amor por él, pero sobre todo su esperanza-
Convinces us that things will be okay.
Things will be okay.

We are sitting in *El Círculo*
A vigil for a patient no longer with us
We are a small group.
It's quiet
I am searching for the words
just seeming to escape me.
They talk

I listen,
Of friends and family
Of borders
Parents who passed away on the other side
While children were away
Who never could return.
These man-made walls that shut us in
They never had proper closure
To hold their fathers
Their mothers as they passed away
These stories are not uncommon.
Yet in your way, you explain that your father is still with you
Siempre.

The men speak of drink,
The comfort sought at the bottom of a bottle
It's expensive and gets us into trouble they say.
He, freshly sober
Battling with these shadows
The death of his girlfriend
Desire to drink and stop the pain
That stalks him daily.

The conversation turns to me,
They ask me if I drink?
So in my best *Pocho* Spanish, I tell them

Pues Sí,
Soy de una familia de alcohólicos
¿Pero los jóvenes toman mucho verdad?
Especialmente los hombres.
They laugh

Pero es importante para mi, que
Siempre cuando estoy tomando
Tengo que pensar
"¿porque estoy tomando?"
¿Me entiendes?

¿ Es solo que yo quiero disfrutar un poco?
O,
¿ Hay algo mas que no quiero sentir,
Hay algo que no quiero ver?

Everything quiet
They nod their heads in acknowledgment

In understanding.

I leave it all in that room
With the *Pan Dulce, El Rosario*
Con Los Flores y La Vela.

'4 walls and a ceiling'

All you need
Everything else a bonus.

Places to go
Things to do
Two feet to take you there
Health
and breath.

So much movement these days
Like coming home
Like a fresh start
Like old toys become new
A second chance
Aimed down the barrel of eternity
In the now.

Heat waves
90's alt music
U-turns
And coffee cups.

Uncertainty and doubt
Changing bodies
Passing times.

Family
Roots and all
Young children growing like branches
A reminder of where we come from
And where we will become again
Just beyond the horizon.

Where stillness speaks
In a glimpse
Reaching
Grasping
Touching
The timeless.

'Touching the Timeless'

I have this daydream waking
I can close my eyes
Even now
And it is with me
More real than any memory.

Black sea
Silent and still
Opaque
Three lone stars reflected
Above boundless night
Intersected by tendrils of luminescent light
Dissipating
In and out
In and out
In and out
Of existence like sullen ash
Boundlessly spreading across to the
Very edge of perspective
Awash in fades and hues of blue
Giving birth to horizon.

Universe
Blinking into existence
We find
Two radiant balls of pure light
Dancing, playing
Endlessly across this shimmering sea
One floats just above and out of reach
At a leisurely yet consistent pace
He the more seasoned and contained of the pair
A darker hue
Like a yellow moon
She dances
Ceaselessly
Above the water
Ever forward
Diving in and out
Dancing along this brim of eternity
Pure joy and weightlessness
A softer
Vibrant yellow

Pulsating gently
Effervescent
Form full and pure.

I could not tell you where life began
Or where it will end
But I imagine it is there
A place beyond time.

Where ripples echo unending
Here in the birthplace of eternity
Where two lights
Dance ceaselessly
Across the endless shimmering sea
Three stars watching
Here in the final resting place, expanse,
Eternity.

'A friend died today'

I held your gaze as you passed
Your eyes a milky tired hue
We knew
You knew
You did not fight it.

I watched you grow up and grow old.
It was cancer
It is always cancer.
I've seen this movie before,
Heard the story
The hero dies in the end.

But,
There are worse things than Death.

You were in pain
How selfish of we to prolong the process?

In truth you lived a long & full life
Loved by many and loving in return.

A beautiful soul
How blessed to have known you
Never a malicious intention in your bones
Source of love and comfort for all that knew you

You went in peace,
You did not go alone.

You are no longer in pain
You are happy wherever you are
Thank you for the lessons you taught my heart
I am so excited to see where the spaces you left in our hearts will take us.

I love you.

'A Note From My brother'

Every day it is the same
This skin is a trap
It's a sick joke
That I know the punchline to
All too well
These joints cracking and grinding
This body is a boneyard.

When I wake up in the morning these hands swollen like tennis balls
I am faced with a choice
Go back to bed and sleep
And sleep
And sleep
Until sleep makes me sick to my stomach
Or take my medication and try to carry on with this day
But some days I don't even want to get out of bed
Wait
That's not true
Not true at all.

Every day
Every day I want to get out of bed
But too many days I can't
I can't and it is killing me
Slowly
Like heart sick
Like god wouldn't things be easier if I wasn't here
Maybe then I could rest
Arthritis is the thief that stole my life from me.

I think of what and how things used to be
Of how they could have been
I make the conscious decision not to take these pharmaceuticals
The pain pills
The Vicodens & Oxycodone
I don't like the way the opiates make me feel
Skin crawling
Rage
It reminds me too much of when I was homeless
Dealing meth out of a storage unit
So I go green
Self-medicating
With the best alternative that I know.

My family

I love them
But I don't know how to tell them that.

It's this chronic pain
Every joint in my body
Swelling and pulsing
With every heartbeat
My central nervous system is screaming
But most of all it's the sadness
This numbing hopelessness mass I am reduced to
Things just keep going wrong
Getting worse and worse
Every time I feel like I take a step forward
Life forces me to take three steps back.

And I get mad
God Damn right I get mad
And I yell
And I scream
I blame my mom
I blame my brother
I even blame the fucking dog
I push those closest to me away.

I think I ran my little brother out of this house
He was the one good thing I ever helped build
I love him.

This life gets lonely
So lonely
I often wonder if life is worth continuing at all.

This is me
On my darkest days
When I want to get out of bed
SO bad
But I can't
And it is killing me.

This a note about my brother
My brother raised me
As a son
The 18 year age difference between us was perfect
We definitely have our differences
But I love that man
He is why I am who I am today
His walk in this life is my inspiration

He is why I want to study medicine
Although I never could fix you
He is why I seek to build with my words and actions
Because I've seen from a first-person perspective the damage they can cause.

For a long time
I did not understand
Mom,
why is this house broken?
Why are there holes in the walls?
Mom,
Why are we yelling?
Mom,
Why are you crying?
Why am I crying?
Mom,
Why are the cops here?
Mom!
Why are they taking my brother away from me?
Mom,
I don't understand
Why is it
We can be fine one moment
But the next we are at each other's throats
I just want to stay in my room and play video games
Things are easier this way.

I turned 18 and left
Thought I might not ever look back
And in a way things were easier
But
The more I ran
These unresolved feelings caught up with me.

'The Place I Call Home'

Where I come from living rooms feel more like battlefields
This drum beat in my chest a silent protest
Where cigarette smoke and overcast skies don't look so different
Where rock bottom is a place called home.

Where I come from we shoot first with our words
Apologizing later
Bones twisted like fiber glass in my throat
Words tinged with regret
Never to be taken back
All of 21 years.

Try to understand how
Where I come from
I did not know myself
Until I destroyed myself
Rebuilding again from the ashes
Brick by brick
So that one of these days roses might bloom from even the saddest parts of myself.

See

I carry this broken music box inside my chest
I wind it up and play all the pretty tunes the girls like to hear
But in the end where I come from
We are all just broken toys
So, when it is all said and done
I'll still be here
Alone
Picking up the pieces.

'Conditions of Circumstance'

There are moments
In life we must
Walk through.

Moments that hurt
Moments that cringe
And cry
And shame.

But we must walk through them all the same
No other cure exists
That I know of.

For these
The conditions of circumstance
Which bind us
Be courageous
Try your best.

What is meant to be
Will
And what is rightfully yours
Already is.

So be brave
Be human
Make mistakes,

And learn to
Try again.

'Billete'

I do not need to travel the entire world

Just to feel the encompassing breadth of humanity

Glimmering along

But

What a show it will be

'Scar Tissue'

Sometimes I read over our old messages
These leftover feelings
That I scrawl out along my bedroom walls

Beautiful portraits of you
In my arms
Everything that went into
We

Acrylic embodiment carved across my rib cage
Your greatest gift
A smile that left me in pieces

When I met you
I closed my eyes
I hoped and dreamed
Yet now
I simply shut my eyes and sigh

I get up off my bed
I throw my phone on the charger
I turn off the light
I leave the writing on the walls
I trace your name along my rib cage
I fall asleep.

'Something Carved and Real'

We all deserve to be with someone who makes us feel special
The one who makes us want to write flower and song into existence
There is something to be said for Consistency
For the one who meets you halfway
For the one who makes them self available
For the one who not only enjoys the idea of you
But the one who does not back away from the real you
The one who pulls on your heart string
Like the moon and her tides.

To the one who keeps you warm in the silence of midnights
Has to leave before daybreak
Initials left carved and real
Along rib cage.

This is for you-
-But also, for me.

To the way you make me feel like I am enough
Like maybe this time I can be part of our solution
There is definitely something to be said about this one
I hope this is a start.

'Mindful Prayers'

I am no carpenter
-But I will build you this home
Here, tucked just below my rib cage
And with these hands
I will paint you a smile
Dancing it across your lips

So why don't you stay awhile?
And listen to my heartbeat
As
We speak our names into dust.

'Less-Than or Equal to Zero'

I feel weighed down
I know I should do
Should go
Should write
I know it could be good for me
But sometimes I just don't
Do

Easier to numb out
But this leaves me feeling unsatisfied
Listless
And full of doubt

I don't feel like I can just be anywhere
The problem isn't me I say
I just don't know
This me now
No this isn't me he says
Like
Out of frequency
Like
Out of alignment

The distractions all around me
In me
Us
All the time

I know that time passes regardless
That things will not always be easy
Nor should they be
Doubt will be present regardless
Weather you follow your dreams
Or not

So I say
Without speaking
Like remembering
Without knowing
Put your heart into the first step
And then the next
Will get you there

Whether you clung to safety
Left unfulfilled
Hungry

35

Safe
Withering on the vine

Somedays feel like I'm just
Surviving
And this is part of life, yes, I know
But I don't want to make a
Home here
In this fear

I guess I hold back because I just don't know
If any of this will make sense
Will it resonate
Will anyone understand
Should they even

I don't like asking for help
Don't like to disappoint
Or feeling less than
Or equal to zero.

'Grandpa Ray'

Grandpa passed away when I was in the third grade
But I remember his presence
Grew up in his home
Recognize the way people admire him
Even today.

But if I could

I'd ask my grandfather his favorite color
Just to remember his voice.

I'd ask him about the war
So, I too could know
What it was like to be strong
When everything is broken.

I'd ask him if he was proud of me
I'd ask him what it means to be a man.

Ask him if I too would ever fall in love one day
And build a family.

I'd ask him why the world hurts so much
Why we break young men down
Instead of teaching them how to fly.

I'd ask him why my brother has trouble walking some days
I'd beg him for a reason.

Just to tell me there's a purpose

Behind
Beyond
The pain.

I'd give my grandfather a crown
Made of seeds
Of all the hopes and dreams of a
Family who Loved him sooooooo much.

Who relied on him
Admired him.

How that was taken away from them.

The miracle of life
Out of death
Learning to grow
&
Walk in our own
Light.

Thank you.

'19'

In recognition of how it felt to be 19
So full of life
Lost
With nowhere to go but Up ↑
I remember
My kingdom in the Sky
Unfolding across silver tinged skyline
Orient gold
Black marble pantheons to the gods
Living sunsets awash in red hues and violet blues
Splitting angel faces across Vatican riverbank.

I remember kissing her
Below our crescent Spanish moon
-The pain of saying goodbye
As the silence of those midnights crowded in on me
I remember being 15 feeling like I was going
No Where Fast-
-Shut my eyes just to rest for a Second
A moment
Awoke in Europe
Crying down the side of Mountains as my denial gave way and I came headlong
Crashing into my past
And yet for the first time in years I could breath.

I Remember
Barcelona bike rides
Criss crossing through traffic
Hurtling down main Street
Like death could never catch me
Valencia festival streets
Firecrackers echoing choruses like a thousand cannon *SHOTS*
Cracking the sky in half like lightning.

-Clarity-

A young man searching for a voice
Shaping it like acrylic steel in flames devouring my sun and stars
It gave birth to a universe all my own
Held together by the consummate gravity of my words.

-Austerity, lost generation, acropolis, gunshots & pickpockets,
A Poet's blood runs cold
Those Parisian streets got soul
Graffiti giving rise to voice abandoned buildings from

Lisbon to ← → Athens
Murals poured out along city walls like love notes
Heard on deaf ears.

I remember
Training my mouth to speak in grandfather's tongue
Searching for words just seeming to escape me
The salsa dancing
And flamenco concerts,
Coming home to the rising sun.
Falling in love in Rome
My heart broken in Florence
Stitched back together again
Along the train tracks to Madrid piece by piece.

Coffee shops, curled up with a book and just reading
For hours rolled into days
As the earth passed me by
Loving every minute of it
Sleeping in train stations halfway across the world
Camel rides, red eye flights, guitar strings,
Budapest barbershops & Amsterdam coffee shops.

I still remember her.

'Cork'

I knew a woman of rain
Whom drew breath within the emerald isle
Flowing Auburn hair cascading across elegant drawn out collarbones
Like Waterfalls
Tracing her embodiment
Radiant beside me
Tender to the touch,
Subduing her
a rebel county
unto muted
Splendor

A tender voice like a wisping fireplace
The crisp coastal breeze kissing me in return
Two travelers pulled across fragmented moments of Eden

Maybe in another lifetime
Down the line
I can hold her

As love so fleeting
Stops to stay awhile.

'Culture Shock'

They told me coming back home would be the hardest part
Waking up feeling empty
The not knowing if my tomorrows
Could live up to my yesterdays.

Culture shock

Not understanding all this emotion
But with not a single ounce of regret
Because I'd do it all again
In a heartbeat.

This deep need tearing me apart.

When I was abroad
I more than anything wanted to come back home
But now that I am here
I need to be anywhere else.

I'm realizing that home is where I build it
And that I still have so much farther to go.

'Recuerdos'

When I was very young my mom and I
Lived in a tiny trailer
In those days
Autumn rain showers were like a blessing.

I carry memories of those rainy days
When
The air smelled of hot chocolate and French
Toast.

When my mom would keep the stove on low
So that it was safe and warm
When the gentle *tap tap* tapping of rain
Drops on our aluminum roof rocked me to
Sleep at night.

Where I awoke to the smell of fresh Atmosphere after rain showers
And mom frying bacon, papas & eggs
I must have been 3 years old.

My best memories
And why I love the Rain.

'Chasing Sunsets'

I have a bit of a type-

Bit on the short side
Morenita, passionate,
Loving to a fault
With eyes like open wounds.

A boy experiencing first love
She broke me down and opened me up to new sides of myself
Taught me what it meant to love another and be loved in return,
Cultivating my compassion of expression
Capacity to feel and be felt.

It was the way she called my name,
-played with my hair
She awakened me to my own yearning heart.

The recognition in her eyes when she knew
That she loved me
Our hearts sinking in the dark well of a movie theater.

Until one day
The cold quite bitter taste when I no longer loved her
If ever at all.

Once she stopped me and said
"Why do you kiss so quickly?
Slow down, what's your rush.
What are you running from?"

Silence of first love broken
An acknowledgement of a future of hollow promises,
Swept under the rug,
Spilled milk,
Forgotten toys.
Like so many other childish things.

'Untitled'

I don't know much
But I know Life
Like love
Is not about taking
It is about sharing.

And love
Like happiness
Appears when we stop chasing it.

Learning to recognize both my pain & privilege
How can I ever be honest with you?
When I haven't been honest with myself.

Leaving those who love me most
On the sidelines,
Chasing what I cannot have
Going no-where fast.

'The War of Art'

Somedays all we have are small victories.

Like
A smile
A cup of coffee
Take the stairs.

Somedays we win the battle
But inside it feels like we lost the war
Somedays we lose
Falling
Crashing
Shattering
Grasping
and drowning
In the depths of pain and shame
Overwhelming
Adversity and doubt
It's the little things that can make all the difference.

But breathe will come
Fresh air fills your lungs
Puts wind in your step
Illuminates the silver lining
A path forward.

Somedays all we have are small victories.

So, enjoy them
Let it wash over you
Where the light has driven out the dark
If only for a moment
The largest of victories are built off a foundation of small ones
And so, we celebrate
Laugh and cheer
We laugh at what incredible power we gave voluntarily
To the shadows that follow us daily
How we let the battle define us
And so, we learn
Slowly
To dust ourselves off.

Then
Let it go.

Because tomorrow brings more battles
More lessons to be learned
And not so small victories.
'Youth in Time of War'

Some days I feel like I am drowning
Choking on my own inabilities
Caught between the man I am and the man I need to be.

Other days I feel a great flame rising up from within this gut
Devouring me
As the sun and all its stars erupt
Cascading streaks across heaven's gate
Scattering me along night skies.

And now I am become soul
Become a verb
Become a man
Made salt & earth
Some days.

But today
Today I am going to succeed
I will succeed when my grit matches the clench of my jaw
The balls of my fists
I am going to succeed when
My need to breath is second to my need to win
To win at all costs
I am going to succeed one day!

But sometimes
Just maybe
Success is not me
Not I - made hammer
Made a fist.

Maybe succeeding means finding my peace
Learning to let go
And let god
As the universe unfolds itself before me like a song

Because in the end what is success truly
If not, simply a line we draw across the sand
Ever changing with the tides.

'Always Running'

A day comes when we must leave home
Like saltwater in the veins they say
Always running.

I can't explain it
Not running from problems
From home
From self
Or
Family.

More like
Leaving to find answers
To continue picking up the pieces
To live a life worth leading
With no regrets
Come home one day.

Different now
More complete than present moment
Balanced, strong, capable, fearless
Whole.

'Gaslight'

It was easier than I thought it would be
To stop talking to you
At least at first.
Even though we lived in the same home
You a ghost in my life.
Leaving for work before I awoke
Coming home from studying long after you'd returned.
It didn't hit me until many months later
There was no going back
This
Hurt much more than I expected.

You took it upon yourself to bend others to your ends
But what I needed was a friend.
You undermined me at every turn
Verbally abused me in front of our friends,
When I spoke my dreams into reality what did you do?
You laughed at me.

The last straw was
When you threatened me with physical violence
Said you were going to
"beat some sense into me"
I left.

Walked away from this friendship
Which felt so much like a chore,
A fight I was never prepared for.

I grew to hate the man you drew out from me
I found myself saying things I didn't really mean
And no amount of your sarcasm will ever make any of this "okay".

In your own way you meant well,
But you and I are too fundamentally different-
-And headstrong.
You were looking for something,
A certain brand of Friend,
Someone to save you
This, I could never be for you.

I pray you a youth caught between his rage & his pain
Learns that these problems cannot be fixed with a fist
And make your peace
Before
All your friends fall away.

'My skin'

I call my skin ugly
I call my skin psoriasis
I call it embarrassing, Disgusting,
I call it Disease
I call my skin Fat
But when was the last time I called my skin beautiful?

This lighter shade of brown a roadmap
Of my unique and shared history,
Why do I often feel that I must prove my "brownness"
Who creates these rules anyway?

My skin is my prison.
But why do I hate my skin for loving me so much?
These red blotches on my face the exclamation point of
All these insecurities painted across my forehead.

A letter to This skin
Which keeps me warm at night
You have always been there for me
And I love you

'Not Entirely Unbroken'

Here the Boy Stands
Young and full of ambition
A belly full
An aching heart
Looking for a reason
Not knowing he is the reason
They send him to school
Sit up
Shut up
Just listen
They tell him
Just do as you are told
Don't ask too many questions
Keep a low profile
And you too can own a pricey car loan
A mortgage, blood pressure pills
Your birthright they call it
Don't rock the boat
Or ask too many questions.

Here the Man Weeps
Alone
Beaten and broken down by this sick world
They tell him he's lost his way
They tell him that he deserved it
That the feeling in his gut
The way things are twisted up inside
They tell him this is his birthright
A man
Nothing more than a body made a gun
They point at him and shame
Where have his dreams gone
He has no time to think
To read
To be
The bills due in full
No time to ask a question
Like how did life ever come to this
Almost as if it was
All by design

Here a Nation Waits Not Entirely Unbroken
For a change to come
For a dream deferred
For full bellies

And strong families
For a touch of compassion
An end to broken men and sullen shoulders
When do we put an end
To the ways
They stole our dreams from us
Rented back to us
What about a new way
Our way
Unbroken

'Yo soy Chicano'

I am a Mexican-American
A walking-talking
Rebellion
All these hypocrisies I call "homeland"
Apart from this red earth
That runs through these veins.
I carry the ghosts of ancestors in my chest
And if you think for an instance
That you will take this away from me
Then you will have to pry it away from my cold dead hands.
-
I am Latino,
I was birthed from struggle and soil and revolutionary fervor.
From oppression and rape
Colonizer and colonized alike.
I will lend my voice and hand to all those whom you seek to persecute
Because you are not my authority you are my oppressor.
And my struggle starts here
-
Aqui Estamos, La Lucha Sigue

'Every day I am afraid'

Afraid that I'll try my hardest and someone will tell me it isn't enough
That I am not enough
Afraid they will slam the door in my face
Afraid one of these days they will realize I don't belong here
In these College classes I feel like an Imposter.

Every day I am Afraid
But I get out of bed to face this day
Once I looked up the definition of courage
"Perseverance in the face of uncertainty and doubt"
Grandmother calls this "Faith"
I think she is on to something.

Every day we deal with this fear of the unknown
I have come so far
I am healthy
My heart is full
And my ambitions untamed
I have so much farther to go
For this too
I am thankful.

They may still try to keep me out of their academia
Slam the door in my face
So I will make a window
And find a way.

'Guanajuato'

Tiene algo especial
Me inspiró a escribir de nuevo.
-

Tal vez sean las estrechas aceras
Callejones iluminados
Túneles subterráneos
O sus altas paredes abrazan el camino por delante
Dando paso a cielo abierto
La bruma mezclado con horizonte de cinta roja.
-

Tal vez sean las interminables colinas onduladas
Sus casas coloridas y enraizadas
Tal vez sea El Pípila
De pie debe vigilando
Tal vez sea El Callejón
Donde los amantes besaron.
-

Tal vez sea las noches muy tardes
La Antigua, Oveja Negra, o Barfly
Cuando el ritmo Reggae pinta las paredes
Nuestras cabezas cabeceando en coro
Los cuatro de la mañana sesiones de salsa
En La Dama de las Camelias .
-

Fue
El hostal en el que me alojé
Un cruce
Un lugar de reunión
Donde la gente de todos los rincones del mundo viene a descansar
A reír
A tomar
Y bailar
Y fiesta
Para ver y ser visto.
-

Un hombre dijo
" Cuando subimos a una montaña
Dejamos allí un pedazo de nosotros mismos,

Y a su vez llevamos una
Pieza de la montaña con nosotros"
Sé que esto es verdad.
Y aún así llevamos una pieza
De cada hostal
Mejor Dicho: De cada persona
Compartimos aliento
Tiempo
Y
Beber.
-

Lo vi
Antes de que lo percibiera
Lo sentí
Antes de entenderlo
Por La Bufa
En La Dama
Alrededor de la mesa de la cocina.
-

En las conversaciones muy nocturnas
Desvelado y obscura
Baile
Y amanecer
Encontré una parte de mí mismo allí
En esa cueva
Entre las montañas.
-

Espero volver
Un día pronto
Lleno
Sin aliento
Y puro.
-

Segundo de Agosto, 2021, Guanajuato
Christian Rivera Nolan

Guanajuato

Tiene algo especial
Inspired me to write again.
-

Maybe it's the narrow sidewalks
Dim lit alleyways
Subterranean tunnels
Or it's towering walls hugging the path ahead
Giving way to open sky
Haze mixed with red ribbon horizon.
-

Maybe it's the endless rolling hills
Their houses colorful and rooted
Maybe it's El Pípila
Standing dutifully a guard
Maybe it's El Callejón
Where the lovers kissed.
-

Maybe it's the late nights past in
La Antigua, Oveja Negra, or Barfly
As Reggae beats paint the walls
Our heads nodding along in rhythm
The four AM salsa dancing sessions
In La Dama de las Camelias .
-

It was
The hostel I stayed at
A crossroad
A meeting place
Where people from all corners of the world come to rest
To laugh
To drink
& dance
& party
To see and be seen.
-

A man once said
" When we climb a mountain
We leave a piece of ourself there,

And in turn we take a piece
Of the mountain with us"
I know this to be true.
And yet we carry a piece
Of every hostel
Mejor Dicho: of every person
We shared breath
Time
&
Drink.
-

I saw it
Before I perceived it
I felt it
Before I understood it
Por La Bufa
En La Dama
Around the kitchen table.
-

In the late night conversations
Sleepless dark
Dance
& sunrise
I found a part of myself there
In that cave
Amongst the mountains
-

I Hope to return
One day soon
Formful
Breathless
& Pure.
-

'Long Way Home'

Young men should travel
To howl at the moon
To find what was lost
What was here all along
Tucked away.

I build a home wherever I go
In the hearts and eyes of strangers
Two ships passing in the night
All alone
Where a man learns what is really important in this life
Of family, friendship, and adventure.

Where the hard days - are still the best days
Everything a lesson.

Where burden becomes life
And breath becomes air.

When the passing of days becomes like the crashing of waves
Streaming, booming, undeniable,
Free
Formless and pure.

A young traveler may awake to find himself in
The lost and found of the world
Among the broken toys and broken men.

Come so far
To other worlds than these
And yet farther yet to go still
I am a Long Way from Home
But I carry family here in my heart.

If you should find yourself awake at night
Restless
There is a peace on the road.

So
Head on
Pack a backpack
And
Go.

Because

We each have one life to give and no playback
Gotta get it right the first time
Tomorrow never promised.

Just stay safe
And have faith
And when the silence of midnight crowds in you
Remember you are never truly alone
No matter how far you may be
From home.

Christian Rivera Nolan studied Biology and Latino/a Studies at San Francisco State University. His experiences growing up in Santa Clara California, to a family conflicted by alcoholism and illness shaped his perspective of the world. He aspires to become a doctor and give back through direct service to underrepresented communities. He enjoys spoken word poetry, film and traveling whenever the opportunity arises. His work has been published in the Acentos Review, Red Earth Review and Edify Fiction.

Made in the USA
Monee, IL
21 April 2022

94918499R00038